# NINJAS

# &

# FIRE DRAGON

# THIS BOOK BELONGS TO

_____

FOR KIDS WHO  WANT TO BECOME NINJA

ISBN: 9798894582788

HIRO AND KENJI TRAINED EVERY MORNING IN THE MISTY MOUNTAINS.
THEIR GRANDFATHER, MASTER JIRO, TAUGHT THEM PATIENCE,
STRENGTH, AND HONOR.

ONE DAY, WHILE PRACTICING NEAR A WATERFALL, KENJI HEARD RUSTLING IN THE BUSHES. HE SIGNALED HIRO TO STAY QUIET AND LISTEN CAREFULLY.

THEY APPROACHED SLOWLY, PEEKING BEHIND THE THICK GREEN LEAVES. TO THEIR SURPRISE, A TINY DRAGON WITH SHIMMERING SCALES LAY CURLED UP.

THE DRAGON HAD BRIGHT GOLDEN EYES AND LET OUT A SMALL BURST OF FLAME.
THEN, IN A BLINK, IT DISAPPEARED INTO THIN AIR!

DID YOU SEE THAT?" KENJI WHISPERED. HIRO NODDED. "A DRAGON THAT CAN TURN INVISIBLE? INCREDIBLE!" THEY LOOKED AROUND, SEARCHING FOR IT AGAIN.

CAREFULLY, HIRO REACHED OUT HIS HAND. SUDDENLY, THE DRAGON
REAPPEARED, SNIFFED HIS FINGERS, AND LET OUT A TINY, WARM PUFF
OF FIRE.

"WE SHOULD TAKE CARE OF IT," KENJI SAID. "BUT WHAT IF SOMEONE DANGEROUS FINDS OUT ABOUT THIS DRAGON?" HIRO WONDERED.

# Ember

THEY DECIDED TO CALL THE DRAGON EMBER.

EACH DAY, THEY TRAINED WITH EMBER, TEACHING IT TO FLY, HIDE, AND CONTROL ITS FIERY BREATH.

MASTER JIRO NOTICED THE BOYS SNEAKING FOOD TO SOMEONE. "WHAT ARE YOU HIDING?" HE ASKED. KENJI HESITATED BUT THEN SHOWED HIM EMBER.

MASTER JIRO GASPED. "A FIRE DRAGON! THEY ARE RARE
AND POWERFUL. YOU MUST PROTECT IT. MANY WILL SEEK TO
CAPTURE ITS MAGIC."

MEANWHILE, IN A DARK FORTRESS, LORD KURO, AN EVIL WARLORD, RECEIVED NEWS OF A RARE DRAGON IN THE MOUNTAINS. HE WANTED IT FOR HIMSELF.

"WITH A FIRE DRAGON, I WILL BE UNSTOPPABLE," KURO
GROWLED. HE SENT HIS BEST WARRIORS TO FIND AND CAPTURE
THE DRAGON.

HIRO, KENJI, AND EMBER TRAINED HARDER. EMBER LEARNED TO TURN INVISIBLE QUICKLY AND SHOOT PRECISE STREAMS OF FIRE. IT GREW STRONGER EVERY DAY.

ONE EVENING, A SHADOW PASSED OVER THEIR CAMP. HIRO LOOKED UP AND SAW WARRIORS IN DARK ARMOR APPROACHING. "THEY'VE FOUND US!" HE WHISPERED

KENJI GRABBED EMBER WHILE HIRO DREW HIS WOODEN TRAINING SWORD. "WE HAVE TO MOVE FAST!" HE SAID. "STAY INVISIBLE, EMBER!"

THE BROTHERS RAN THROUGH THE DENSE FOREST, DODGING BRANCHES AND LEAPING OVER ROCKS. EMBER FLICKERED IN AND OUT OF SIGHT, STRUGGLING TO STAY HIDDEN.

KURO'S WARRIORS CHASED THEM ON HORSEBACK. "FIND THE DRAGON!" ONE
SHOUTED. THE BROTHERS KNEW THEY COULDN'T OUTRUN THEM FOREVER.

THEY REACHED A NARROW CLIFFSIDE. "NOW WHAT?" KENJI ASKED. HIRO TOOK A DEEP BREATH. "WE MAKE OUR STAND HERE."

THE WARRIORS SURROUNDED THEM. "HAND OVER THE DRAGON," THEIR LEADER DEMANDED. "NEVER!" HIRO SHOUTED, GRIPPING HIS SWORD TIGHTLY.

EMBER SUDDENLY APPEARED, EYES GLOWING FIERCELY. IT LET OUT A POWERFUL BURST OF FIRE, FORCING THE WARRIORS TO STEP BACK IN SURPRISE.

KENJI AND HIRO FOUGHT BRAVELY, USING THEIR TRAINING TO DODGE AND COUNTER
THE WARRIORS' ATTACKS. EMBER SWOOPED AND STRUCK WITH FIERY BLASTS.

MASTER JIRO ARRIVED, HIS STAFF GLOWING WITH ENERGY. "YOU WILL NOT TAKE THE DRAGON!" HE DECLARED, STANDING BETWEEN THE BOYS AND THE WARRIORS

WITH A MIGHTY STRIKE, MASTER JIRO SENT THE WARRIORS STUMBLING BACK. EMBER UNLEASHED A FINAL FIRESTORM, FORCING THEM TO FLEE.

DEFEATED, THE WARRIORS RETURNED TO LORD KURO. "THE DRAGON IS TOO POWERFUL," THEY REPORTED. KURO CLENCHED HIS FISTS IN RAGE.

: "THIS ISN'T OVER," KURO VOWED. BUT FOR NOW, THE BROTHERS AND EMBER WERE SAFE. THEY NEEDED A NEW HIDING PLACE.

MASTER JIRO LED THEM TO A SECRET VALLEY, HIDDEN BY MIST. "HERE, EMBER WILL BE SAFE AND CAN GROW STRONGER," HE SAID.

EMBER NUZZLED THE BROTHERS, GRATEFUL FOR THEIR PROTECTION. IT WAS TIME TO TRAIN HARDER, TO PREPARE FOR WHATEVER CAME NEXT.

DAYS TURNED INTO WEEKS. THE BROTHERS HONED THEIR SKILLS WHILE EMBER PRACTICED FLYING HIGHER AND CONTROLLING ITS FLAMES.

ONE EVENING, EMBER SOARED ABOVE THE VALLEY, ROARING TRIUMPHANTLY. IT HAD GROWN STRONGER AND MORE CONFIDENT, READY FOR ANY DANGER.

HIRO AND KENJI SMILED. "WE WILL ALWAYS PROTECT YOU," KENJI SAID. EMBER LET OUT A BURST OF FIRE, LIGHTING UP THE NIGHT SKY.

www.ingramcontent.com/pod-product-compliance
Lightning Source LLC
Chambersburg PA
CBHW081749200326
41597CB00024B/4452